Your Wall or Mine?

The Party Wall etc. Act 1996
A Simplified Guide

Mr Dil Gujral, BA (Hons), MFPWS

Best Wishes. Eugene

Thank you for your

support.

D S G

To place an order please go to:

1996 Party Wall Ltd

(www.1996PartyWall.co.uk)

Or e-mail: info@1996PartyWall.co.uk

ISBN: 9781796278361

First published 2019

3

Preface

I am a Party Wall Surveyor with over 10 years' experience in the field dealing with projects ranging from simple extensions to a variety of complex commercial projects.

I have had various careers, the majority of which have involved working in the Construction industry in some shape or form. Party Wall Surveying is the most interesting so far as it involves dealing with people of varying mindsets and thought processes.

Working as a Specialist Party Wall Surveyor I find myself explaining the issues contained in this book repeatedly. Unfortunately, lack of time and complexity of the subject matter do not help. Therefore I have tried to explain this important subject in a simplified manner in order to help the reader gain a better understanding.

The reader will gain a better understanding of the purpose of The Party Wall etc. Act 1996 ("The Act") and how it's likely to affect them if they are Owners of any type of property in England or Wales (The Act does not apply to Scotland or Northern Ireland). This includes Property Investors, Property Developers, Home Owners and anyone likely to be affected by the building works.

The Act actually came into effect on 1st July 1997

Contents

Introduction

Your Wall or Mine ?

This is the second most common question normally asked by property owners. Normally property owners think about their property in terms of the legal boundary.

Party Wall law works differently; property owners should think about the Party Wall as the total width belonging to both owners simultaneously. This is analogous to children having two parents simultaneously.

This concept is sometimes misunderstood by Planners who fail to understand the term "Curtilage", especially where Lofts are involve raising the Party Wall. The Act also applies to other types of works hence the "etc." in the title. This includes excavation within defined distances.

This book will give the reader a better understanding of The Act and how it might apply to their circumstances.

Building Owners Section

CHAPTER 1

Building Owners' Perspective

When Party Wall Surveyors discuss The Act, they talk about Notices and Section numbers. This does not necessarily mean a lot to Property Owners, Builders and anyone else involved who may be thinking in terms of their project. Therefore, I tired to relate examples of projects to the relevant Sections within The Act. Examples of projects are:

- Rear Extension
- Loft Extension / Loft Conversion
- Removal of Chimneys
- Basements

\-   Porches

The Building Owner Section is written from the viewpoint of the project first and then mapped to the Notices and Sections of The Act.

The Adjoining Owner Section is written from the perspective of any potentially affected parties. Adjoining Owners are likely to receive a Section Notice which may be accompanied by a description of the works and drawings.

The Act came into force on 1st July 1997 and applies to all properties, commercial or residential, throughout England and Wales only. The Act is not applicable to Scotland or Northern Ireland.

The purpose of The Act is to ensure Building Owners are able to carry out building works within a mechanism for resolving any disputes that arise without the need to go to court as it provides an recognised dispute resolution process.

The Act has the dual purpose of enabling building work to take place and to ensuring that the Adjoining Owner's property is protected.

Planning, Building Control, Boundary Disputes and The Party Wall Act are all elements of property law and each has it's own place - one does not exclude another. In other words, if a property owner has Planning Permission or intends to carry out building works via Permitted Development, it does not mean that they are covered under The Act and that they do not have to undertake the Party Wall process.

The Act applies to **all** properties in England and Wales whether they are commercial or residential. The Act requires the Building Owner to take full responsibility for following The Act and this cannot be delegated to Builders or Project Managers. This is similar to Health and Safety and other laws where the Building Owner has the ultimate responsibility.

CHAPTER 2

Process Overview

In this chapter will give you an overview of the Party Wall process and how it fits into a building project. Once planning has been submitted you should start the Party Wall process.

On completion of the Party Wall process, the build can be commenced. Of course, it is possible to commence the build where the works are not notifiable or start the non-notifiable element of the works.

It is better to ensure that the Party Wall process is either running or completed. During or on completion of the build, occasionally, there may be damage to the Adjoining property. This is where you will go into the post works Party Wall Process. Just to repeat, this is **only** if damage occurs to the Adjoining property.

Let's have a look at the Party Wall process. The first stages are to analyse and create notices.

So, we look at the proposed building works and carry out an analysis of the notifiable works and how it's likely to affect your neighbours. We then create the notices, which are Served to the relevant Adjoining Owners.

The Party Wall Process - Overview

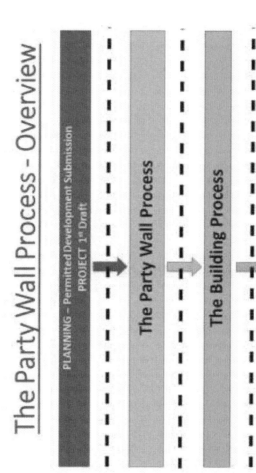

PLANNING – Permitted Development Submission
PROJECT 1st Draft

The Party Wall Process

The Building Process

Post Works – Party Wall Process –
If Damage Occurs to Adjoining Owner Property

The main element of the Party Wall process depends on the response received from your Adjoining Owners.

The Adjoining Owners have three options.

1. They can consent and request a Schedule of Condition (SoC) Survey.
A Schedule of Condition is actually there to protect people carrying out the building works offering protection from false and/or malicious damage claims. This is analogous to renting a car, where the car rental company takes photographs to log any existing damage before it goes out to you.

2. The next option the Adjoining Owner has is to use an Agreed Surveyor i.e. use the same Surveyor as you such that both Building Owner and Adjoining Owner are using the same Surveyor.

3. The third option for the Adjoining Owner is to appoint their own Surveyor. In this case there are

two Surveyors, the Building Owner has a Surveyor and Adjoining Owner has their own Surveyor.

4. The fourth option is not really an option, but does occur on a regular basis. This is when the Adjoining Owner takes no action having received the notice.

The Party Wall (PW) - Process

**Party Wall (PW) –
Analysis Create and Serve Notice**

**Adjoining Owner (AO) –
Response - Options**

1. Consent With Schedule of Condition- SoC

2. Agreed Surveyor BO – AO Use Same Surveyor

3. AO Appoint Own Surveyor

4. AO – Do Nothing The 10(4) Process

We will now look at the process to be followed for each of response in turn:

Option 1. Adjoining Owner consented with a Schedule of Condition

We make an appointment to view and carry out a Schedule of Condition on the Adjoining Owner's property.

We carry out the survey which is largely photographic. The photographs from the survey are held on file in case of future claims.

We also produce a written report known as Schedule of Condition report. This report is sent to both the Adjoining Owner and the Building Owner.

Adjoining Owners Response
1. Consent - with Schedule of Condition- (SoC)

1. Make Appointment With Adjoining Owner (AO)

→

2. Carry – Out Survey on Adjoining Owner's Property

→

3. Produce – Schedule of Condition (Soc) Report

→

4. Send – SoC Report Schedule of Condition To Both Owners – AO & BO

Option 2. Agreed Surveyor is Appointed

If the Adjoining Owner appoints the Agreed Surveyor option whereby the same survey acts for both Building and Adjoining Owner; this is permitted under the Act.

On most occasions, with the exception of basement works, the process is as follows:

We will make an appointment with the Adjoining Owner to inspect their property.
We will carry out a survey of their property. To record the current condition. This is largely a photographic survey.

The next step is to produce a report for the photographic survey; known as the Schedule of Condition report. We also produce a legal document called a 'Party Wall Award' and the Schedule of Condition report forms a part of the Award.

The Award is a legal document, which sets out Rights and Responsibilities of each party.

The last step is to Serve the Award to both the Adjoining Owner and the Building Owner.

Adjoining Owners Response
2. Agreed Surveyor – Both BO & AO Use The Same Surveyor

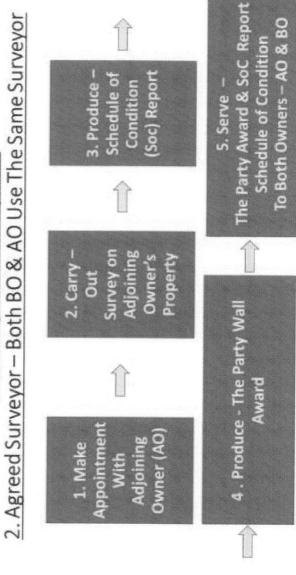

1. Make Appointment With Adjoining Owner (AO)

2. Carry – Out Survey on Adjoining Owner's Property

3. Produce – Schedule of Condition (Soc) Report

4. Produce - The Party Wall Award

5. Serve – The Party Award & SoC Report Schedule of Condition To Both Owners – AO & BO

Option 3. Adjoining Owner Appoints Own Surveyor

The third option for Adjoining Owners is to appoint their own Surveyor; they are allowed to do so under the Act.

In most cases, the Building Owner will be responsible for Surveyor's reasonable fees/costs. The Building Owner appoints their own Surveyor and the Adjoining Owner appoints their own Surveyor.

The first task the two Surveyors need to do is to select a Third Surveyor who will only get involved if called upon by the two Surveyors or either of the owners.

The Adjoining Owner Surveyor arranges an appointment for a Schedule of Condition Survey. The Building Owner Surveyor carries out that Survey in conjunction with Adjoining Owner Surveyor and produces a draft report.

The Building Owners Surveyor also produces a draft Party Wall Award which is a Legal document setting out Rights and Responsibilities of both parties.

Both these documents are then sent to the Adjoining Owner's Surveyor to review and comment upon.

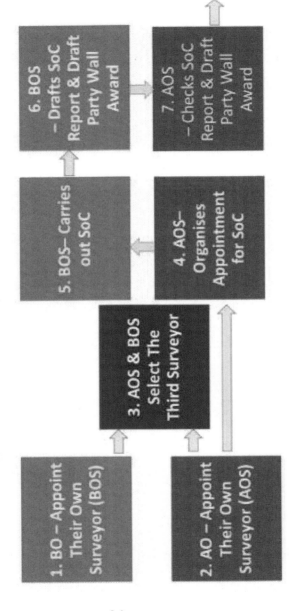

1. BO – Appoint Their Own Surveyor (BOS)

2. AO – Appoint Their Own Surveyor (AOS)

3. AOS & BOS Select The Third Surveyor

4. AOS– Organises Appointment for SoC

5. BOS– Carries out SoC

6. BOS – Drafts SoC Report & Draft Party Wall Award

7. AOS – Checks SoC Report & Draft Party Wall Award

The Adjoining Owner's Surveyor will comment upon the Party Wall Award and the Schedule of Condition Survey report. The Building Owner Surveyor responds to these comments and this can go back and forth for several iteration until agreement is reached.

It is common for the Adjoining Owner Surveyor to request amendments to drawings, Method statements and other documentation. The Building Owner Surveyor requests these from the designers and architects and then passes them onto the Adjoining Owner Surveyor.

Both the Adjoining Owner Surveyor and Building Owner Surveyor agree the Party Wall Award and the Schedule of Condition. Once agreed, these are then signed by both the Building Owner Surveyor and the Adjoining Owner Surveyor.

The Building Owner Surveyor Serves the documents to the Building Owner and the Adjoining Owner Surveyor Serves the Documents to the Adjoining Owner.

Adjoining Owners Response
3. AO – Appoints their Own Surveyor

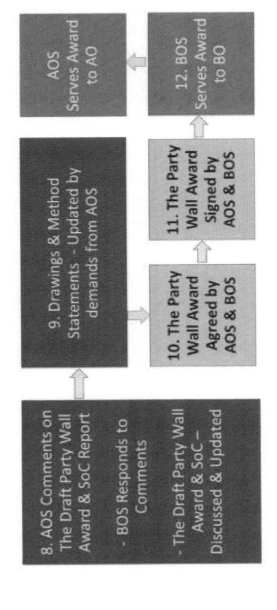

8. AOS Comments on The Draft Party Wall Award & SoC Report

- BOS Responds to Comments

- The Draft Party Wall Award & SoC – Discussed & Updated

9. Drawings & Method Statements - Updated by demands from AOS

10. The Party Wall Award Agreed by AOS & BOS

11. The Party Wall Award Signed by AOS & BOS

AOS Serves Award to AO

12. BOS Serves Award to BO

Option 4. Adjoining Owner Does Not Respond

Where the Adjoining Owner has effectively selected the fourth option by not acting on the notice, it is deemed to be a dispute after 14 + 1 days to allow for postage. We usually allow 16 days.

The next step is that we send a reminder letter, giving them 10 plus 2 days for postage. If there is still no reply:

The Building Owner **MUST** and I repeat **MUST** appoint a Surveyor on their behalf to act for them.

Prior to the appointment of a Surveyor, the Adjoining Owner may reply to the letters choosing one of the three options as follows:

(1) Consenting with a Schedule of Condition
(2) Using an Agreed Surveyor
(3) Appointing their own Surveyor

The Adjoining Owner is not allowed to frustrate the process by not replying to the Party Wall Notice.

Adjoining Owners Response
4. AO – Do Nothing The 10(4) Process

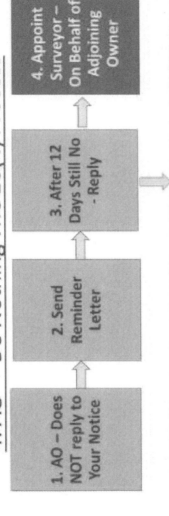

1. AO – Does NOT reply to Your Notice

2. Send Reminder Letter

3. After 12 Days Still No - Reply

4. Appoint Surveyor – On Behalf of Adjoining Owner

3.1 AO Reply's by Selecting An Option
1. - Consent With Schedule of Condition- SoC
2. - Agreed Surveyor BO – AO Use Same Surveyor
3. - AO Appoint Own Surveyor

CHAPTER 3

Adjoining Owner Responses

Under the Party Wall process, the Adjoining Owner cannot stop works proposed by the Building Owner. All they can do is to Appoint a Party Wall Surveyor to represent their interests. It is their Surveyor's duty to help determine the Time and Manner in which the works are carried out. An Adjoining Owner can respond to a notice in the following manner.

1. They can consent to the works and it's usually a good idea to carry out a Schedule

of Condition Survey on the Adjoining Owner's property. This will protect the Building Owner from false and malicious claims of damage which may already exist unbeknown to the Building Owner.

2. They can dissent to the works / Notice and appoint their own Surveyor to represent their interest. The two Surveyors will then determine how the works are carried out in order to minimise the impact on the Adjoining Owner or their property.

3. The Adjoining Owner may dissent but agree to use the same Agreed Surveyor who has to act impartially in order to ensure that the act is administered without favour.

Where you have each owner appointing their Own Surveyors, one of the first duties the two Surveyors undertake is to Select a Third Surveyor. The role of the Third Surveyor will be explained in a separately.

The appointment of Surveyors must be in writing and cannot be rescinded once appointed.

The other type of response Adjoining Owners undertake is a non-response. i.e. they do not reply to Notice Letters. In this situation, the Building Owner should follow the process by sending a reminder letter after 14+1 days. If there is no response to this letter then under Section 10(4)(b) of The Act, after 10+1 days, the Building Owner should appoint a Surveyor on the Adjoining Owner's behalf.

This process, although incurring slightly higher costs for the Building Owner, ensures that they are protected by following the process in The Act and that the building works are not interrupted midstream.

CHAPTER 4

Common Types of Building Works

These could be Residential i.e. owned by residential owners or residential property owned by Buy-To-Let property owners; or Commercial.

Either way the most common type of building works carried out are:

     - Loft conversions / Loft extensions

     - Rear extensions

     - Taking out old chimneys. These could be the Chimney Breast, the chimney element below the roofline or the chimney stack, which is the chimney above the roofline.

- Basements

- Porches

Most of these works are Notifiable to Adjoining Owners. However, this depends on the nature of the work proposed and the position and the distance of the Adjoining Owners' properties.

Some other factors to consider include the ownership of the Adjoining Owners' properties. Things to consider are:

- Whether the neighbour's property is a house or a house that has been converted into flats.

- Whether the property is detached, semi-detached or terraced.

- Other factors also include whether the flat owners are also the freehold owners and the length of lease the properties.

Who to Serve Notices to - Types of Notices

This all depends on the type of works being carried out. Building Owners should consider serving notices as soon as their project is submitted for Planning approval, especially if they are proposing to undertake the works under Permitted Development. This means that they are likely to be doing the works without the need for Planning permission approval.

Who the notifiable owners are depends on:

- The type of project

- The location of your property

- The location of neighbouring properties in relation to yours

- Ownership neighbouring properties i.e. Freehold or Leasehold

- Whether a neighbouring property is a single house or a house split into two or more flats.

- If they are flats then whether the owners are leasehold owners or freehold owners. In certain circumstances, freehold owners can also be leasehold owners.

- In the case of leasehold owners anyone with a leasehold of more than one year is notifiable; therefore, short term leaseholders are excluded. This means leasehold owners of more than one year are also notifiable owners.

All these factors are looked at in conjunction with your project to decide who are the Notifiable owners.

Serving Notice on the correct Adjoining Owners is important. There have been occasions where Building Owners have served Notices themselves and have served notices on too many owners, some of which were not notifiable. This has meant extra expense and delay for those Building Owners.

On the other hand, on occasions, Building Owners have not served all the Adjoining Owners and this has led to their project delays mid construction while the Party Wall issues are resolved.

Therefore, it is extremely important that Notices are served in the correct Manner to the right Adjoining Owners in order to ensure your building project can start and progress without any issues relating to Party Wall matters.

CHAPTER 5

Rear Extension Section Six Notice.

One of the most common types of work is a rear extension. Most rear extensions will need a Section 6 Notice under The Act. Section 6(1) to be exact, which is Served in order to be able to excavate for foundations and lay drainage.

The test to see if a section 6(1) notice is required or not comes in two parts.

- Firstly, whether the excavation is within 3 metres of the Adjoining Property. The 3 metres is measured horizontally at ground level.

- Secondly, whether the excavation is going to a lower level compared to the original foundations of the Adjoining Property within 3 metres.

There is also a section 6(2) notice that is more likely to be applicable to basements and works where the excavations are deeper.

The next question to consider:

- How do I know the depth of my neighbours' building foundations?

Following the heat wave of 1976 some buildings showed cracking in the foundations due to foundations being quite shallow. The Building Control Regulations were updated following this so that buildings must have a deeper foundation.

Therefore if the building was built before 1976, it is likely that the foundations will be very shallow and hence they will be notifiable if they are within 3 meters.

If in doubt, it is better to serve a notice in order to avoid delays and disruption to your project. The range of building dates that this applies to is 1976 to 1980. Buildings constructed from 1980 onwards are likely to have a deeper foundation, therefore may not be notifiable; at least under Section 6(1).

If in doubt, it is better to Serve a Notice, especially if your property is a terraced house.
It is likely that the owners of buildings on both sides will be notifiable. Who the notifiable owners are will be discussed in detail separately but briefly:

If it is a terraced house and you are building a rear extension you have two Adjoining buildings that are notifiable assuming that the excavations are within 3 meters.

The ownership of these buildings depends on how the buildings are structured. If they are flats at ground level then both the leaseholder and freeholder are notifiable.

In the case of semi-detached houses, the house that is attached will definitely be notifiable. On the other side, where there is a distance between the two properties and occupied by a driveway, this is normally approximately 2.40m. If both your property and the Adjoining Owner's property have a driveway then the distance is likely to be greater than 3 meters hence may not be notifiable. Distance are measured at the ground level horizontally.

If the Adjoining property has been converted into flats or is a block of flats, the lease on the ground level will be notifiable as well as the freeholders of the building.

On the other side of a semi-detached property, if the house is within three metres and it has been converted into flats, then both the leaseholder of the ground floor level and the freeholder are notifiable.

Where there is a shed or a garage next to the house and the shed/garages is within three metres of your excavation. Whether the shed is a notifiable structure depends on whether it has a foundation. If it is a wooden shed just sitting at ground level then there are no foundations and hence it is not notifiable. If it is a wooden shed sitting on a slab of concrete, it counts as a foundation and hence it is notifiable.

Again, if in doubt you should Notify.

If you have a semi-detached or a detached house and the original adjoining house is within three metres but an extension has been added. The neighbour's extension is likely to have deeper foundations than the original properties. You will still need to measure beyond the new extension to see if the original structure building is within three metres, in which case it is still notifiable.

If you have a detached house, the adjoining house may also be detached. If it is within three metres of your excavation, the owners of that building are notifiable. Again, if it is split into flats, the leaseholders and freeholders are also notifiable.

For emphasis, if a building has been built since the original house and the original house is within three metres, the owners of that building are notifiable. If they are flats then both freehold and the leasehold owners are notifiable.

If you are building a rear extension and are connecting the extension to the original house by removing a rear wall then this may involve insertion of steel beams or box/goalposts into the Party Wall. This will require either cutting into the Party wall or fixing into the Party wall and therefore is notifiable under Section 2 of The Act.

A Section 6 Notice is notifiable with a One Month notice period, which can be decreased if the Adjoining Owners agree.

A Section 2 Notice is notifiable with a Two Month notice period and again, this can be decreased if the Adjoining Owners agree.

For extensions, Section One Notices may also need to be issued. This is discussed in the "Section One" chapter below.

CHAPTER 6

Rear Extensions - Section One of The Act

Where the proposed project is a Rear Extension, Section One of The Act needs to be considered. This Section deals with building on the Line of Junction. This is simply the boundary at the ground level where the land of the two owners meet.

The Boundary is not defined by the Party Wall Surveyors. This is a separate issue which needs to be agreed by each landowner and can be a complex issue. In terms of The Act and the Line of Junction Notice, there are three further subsections to Section One:

Section 1(5) is the most commonly used, where a Building Owner is building up to the Line of Junction. In this case foundations do not project over the Boundary. Projecting anything over the Boundary such as footings or fascias, would become a trespass which can be a complex issue.

In this scenario, the footings are usually eccentric foundations i.e. the wall is built to the edge of the footings. These are not traditional footings which project beyond the wall.

Section One is the most helpful section of the act for two reasons.

Firstly, if there is no reply within 14+1 days of the notice being Served, it is an automatic consent, i.e. it is deemed that the neighbour has agreed, compared to the other notices, where dissent is automatic after 14+1 days.

Secondly, where a Section One Notice is Served, the Adjoining Owner must grant access to their land for the purpose of carrying out notifiable works under The Act.

In projects, where you are building on the Line of Junction, placing of hoarding and scaffolding on the neighbours land in order to carry out the works is permissible. This is particularly useful where the building is two storeys or higher and scaffolding needs to be erected in order to complying with Health and Safety regulations.

This method of construction also has advantages for both parties. The side wall is easier to build because suitable access is available to undertake pointing work on brick work or to render the wall. As a result, a visually pleasing wall with a better finish to the building is achieved.

Section 1(2) is used to Build Astride the Boundary. For example if you are planning to build an extension and your neighbours are also planning to build a similar extension, then both parties can share a Party Wall. This would result in financial benefits due to the saving in construction costs and would also result in marginally bigger extension due to the saving in land that would otherwise have been used by the second wall.

Usually, one neighbour will build their extension before the other one and hence incur the costs of building the wall.

A neighbour then uses this flank wall later to form their extension. The neighbours can agree whatever they like, however there is a default position set out by The Act. Where there is no agreement for recovery of costs by the first owner to build the wall, it is covered under Section 11(11) making use of costs, commonly known as "Enclosure Costs".

Under Section 11(11) making use of costs allows half the costs the new Party Wall to be recovered by the owner who built the wall.

This payment is only calculated at the point of enclosure i.e. when the second neighbour use this wall to create an extension. There are cases where owners have already paid for part of the wall construction cost as soon as it was built, before making use of the wall as part of the their extension. This is fine but this is not required by The Act.

The recoverable construction costs of the wall are based on costs at the time of enclosure. So regardless of costs at the time of construction, the enclosure costs will be calculated at the point when the wall is actually used.

Section 1(6) covers placing projected footings on land.

However, if you are placing footings on a neighbour's land, this is trespass unless this has been agreed with the neighbour. In this case, the permission to place projecting footings on the

Adjoining Owner's land should be obtained in writing.

It is perfectly possible to build walls on an eccentric foundation, subject to those foundations being sufficient. Therefore, there is no need to use Section 1(6) as Section 1(5) can be used instead with changes to the design of the proposed footings.

CHAPTER 7

Loft Extensions or Loft Conversions

These seem to be the most popular type of works at the moment, probably because home owners are able to add an extra one or two bedrooms to their property; be they flats or houses.

Although each Loft Conversion project is unique, the most common factor is the insertion of steel into the Party Wall in order to gain floor separation for the purposes of sound insulation.

This type of work is notifiable under Section 2(2)(f) of The Act and requiring a Section Three (3) Notice. The normal notice period is two months which can be decreased with the agreement of the Adjoining Owners.

Other works are also notifiable; for example insertion of flashing into the adjoining property.

Another type of notifiable work is the removal of old plaster from the Party Wall.

At the same time, it is also a good idea to Notify the Adjoining Owners of "Weather protection to the Party Wall" i.e. if the two properties in the roof space are joined by a Party Wall, if the roof is removed during the build the Party Wall may be exposed and may require weather proofing for a temporary period.

Weather proofing the Party Wall while the works are being carried out is advisable, as an exposed wall can lead to damp travelling down the wall and affecting properties of all owners.

In some loft projects, Party Walls are raised in order to form dormer cheeks i.e. side of the walls of the loft conversion in order to gain extra space. This is permitted under Section 2 of the Act and notifiable via a Section 3 Notice. However, there can be Planning issues as not all planners understand the term "Curtilage".

This is not the first time Planners have misinterpreted planning law. A similar situation occurred when restrictions for porches first came into the Planning regimen. Planners assumed the Permitted Development allowance included the area for porches, whereas this allowance actually has a separate class of it's own.

Although you are permitted to raise a Party Wall according to Planning law, Planners can still object and thus reject the application. The Building Owner is likely to win an appeal if lodged, this leads to a delay and often they choose to not raise the full Party Wall.

It is usually better to raise the full Party Wall rather than half the Party Wall i.e. only up to the boundary.

The Party Wall should be raised in brick work hence has the following advantages:

- Has a longer lifetime
- Is easier to maintain
- Neighbours are able to make use of it

Once a Party Wall has been raised and a neighbour makes use of it, Section (11)(11) of The Act applies. Here, the neighbour has to pay a contribution towards the cost of construction of the area of the wall being used.

Cost of construction under Section (11)(11) "making use of costs" are calculated based on costs at the time of making use.

CHAPTER 8

Porches

Porches are an interesting topic. Whether a porch is a Notifiable piece of work under The Act depends on several factors.

Firstly, the depth of the proposed foundations.

Secondly, the proximity of the neighbouring property and its make-up and whether the foundations are deeper than the neighbour's foundation. In the case of houses build pre 1976 to 1980, the foundations are fairly shallow. If the neighbour's foundations are within three metres of your excavation, then the porch project will be notifiable under Section Six 6(1)

Therefore, it may be possible to create a slab foundation where the excavation is not very deep and hence unlikely to go below your neighbour's foundation. The second test of excavation within three metres of your neighbours' foundations would then become redundant. Most porch projects are unlikely to cause damage to the neighbouring property.

The other issue to be mindful of is that of boundaries and going beyond your the boundary line.

A Section 1(5) Notice may also be applicable if you are planning to build up to the Line of Junction.

CHAPTER 9

Non-Reply to Your Notice

It is quite common for Adjoining Owners not to reply to Notices Served by Building Owners. This can be for several reasons:

- They are away on holiday.
- They are busy.
- They have forgotten to do it.
- They do not understand it.
- They are trying to frustrate the building works.

Some neighbours believe by not replying to a Party Wall Notice, the Building Owner cannot start their project. However, The Act is there to help Building Owners to carry out their works.

Hence there is provision in the Act to deal with the non-reply of Notices. This is covered under Section 10 of the Act. Simply put, if after 14 + 1 day allowed for postage, the Adjoining Owner has not responded, the Notice is Deemed to have been Served.

If there is no reply then a dispute is deemed i.e. it is understood/implied that the Adjoining Owner has not consented to the works. Disputes are settled by Surveyors who produce an Award to settle matters in dispute relating to the notifiable works.

Once a correctly drafted Notice is Served and there is no reply after 14 + 1 day, it is deemed a dispute.

The next step the Building Owner should take is to send a reminder letter to the Adjoining Owner and ensure the service is documented by obtaining a Certificate of Posting (CoP).

This is known as a "10 day letter" in the industry. Once this is Served, the Adjoining Owners have 10

+ 1 day to reply, assuming this letter has been posted.

It is prudent to allow an extra day, therefore 11 or 12 days after a non-reply, the Building Owner **Must**, I repeat **Must** appoint a different Surveyor on behalf of the Adjoining Owner. This point is often misunderstood Property Professionals, Property Developers and even Solicitors.

The two Surveyors then go on to make an Award, which ensures that the Building Owner is protected by following the process.

Building Owner are sometimes hesitant in doing this because appointing another Surveyor means additional Surveyor fees/costs. However, this is the correct process under The Act which must be followed.

The Adjoining Owner cannot then appoint someone else as their Surveyor therefore, delaying the works midstream. The importance of this part of the process cannot be overstated as delays in construction can cause the building costs to escalate, especially if the Adjoining Owner's motivation is to attempt to frustrate the building works.

CHAPTER 10

Surveyors Fees /Costs - Who Pays & Why?

This is almost the $64,000 dollar question. The answer is:

The Surveyors fees/costs are determined by the Surveyors in making their Award – under "any other matters".

The method used to deciding who pays the Surveyors fees/costs is to consider who benefits from the proposed works. If the proposed works are a Rear Extension, Loft Conversion and Removal of a Chimney breast; it is likely that the Building Owner will gain ALL the benefit and therefore, it is only fair and right that the Building Owner pays all the fees/costs of the Surveyors including that of the Adjoining Owners Surveyors.

The same applies when the Building Owner has appointed a Surveyor on behalf of the Adjoining Owner under Section 10(4)(b) due to non-reply of the Party Wall Notice.

On the other hand, there are instances where works have to be carried out as a result of poor maintenance. For example, the repair of a chimney stack which is the element above the roof line and the tiles, may be required as part of the works.

The Chimney Stack may have become dilapidated due to poor maintenance and is a common outlet for a number of properties owned by a number of Owners. As an example, a chimney stack may be positioned so that there are two flats on one side and a house on the other side. In this case the works will be carried out by one owner but will benefit the other owners.

This will include costs for the repair works; appointing the Surveyors; Professional fees etc. These would usually be apportioned between all three Owners.

A similar scenario also applies to boundary walls where a Party Wall separates the land of two Owners and the wall requires repairs.

Depending on the type and cost of the of project, recovering costs from the various owners may be difficult.   If the costs are minimal then often it is easier and cheaper for the Building Owner to carry out the works at their cost.

Adjoining Owner Section

CHAPTER 11

Introduction – Adjoining Owner (AO)

The Building Owner Section has a perspective of the project first and then translated into the Notices and Sections of The Act. In this section we will look at the Party Wall process from the perspective of an Adjoining Owner.

The Party Wall etc. Act 1996 ("The Act") came into law on 1st July 1997 and unlike Planning, it is not retrospectively enforceable.

The Act has a long history under the London building Act spanning 300 years. Most people are familiar with Building Control, Planning and so forth which were elements of the London Building Act 1939. The Act contains the elements the London Building Act which were previously omitted when the Planning and Building Control Legislation was applied to England and Wales .

The purpose of The Act is to help Building Owners build and to also offer protection to the Adjoining Owners, without the need to go to court.

Adjoining Owners are likely to receive a Section Notice and this may be accompanied by a description of the works and drawings.

Normally, when Party Wall Surveyors discuss The Act, it is in terms of Notices and Section numbers. This does not translate to property owners, builders and home owners who are think in terms of their project. Most common examples of projects include:

- Rear Extension
- Loft Extension / Loft Conversion
- Removing Chimneys
- Basements
- Porches

Most frequently used Notices include:
- Section One (1) Line of Junction works,
- Section Two (2) Works to the Party Wall
- Section Six (6) Excavation works.

The following terms are use and their definitions will be provided later in this book:

- The Building Owner

- The Adjoining Owner

- The Party Wall Surveyor and most importantly

- The Third Surveyor, whose roll causes much confusion

Once a Building Owner decides to carry out building works or repair works which are Notifiable under The Act, they will need to issue Party Wall Notices in order to invoke The Act.

The Act is a legal requirement and it is the Building Owner's responsibility to ensure that all aspects of The Act are complied with.

The Act only comes into play once Notices are Served and it is the Building Owner's responsibility to ensure the Notices are Served correctly. Usually Building Owners engage Party Wall Surveyors to issue Notices and at this point, the Party Wall Surveyor would Serve the Notices as an agent of the Building Owner.

Appointments of the Party Wall Surveyors can begin only once a Dispute has arisen. The Party Wall Surveyors' Appointment is a Statutory Appointment, which means there is no client relationship. All appointments must be in writing and cannot be rescinded.

Party Wall Surveyors must administer The Act fairly and impartially and as such cannot do the bidding of their owners.

A Dispute under the Act may be deemed when an Adjoining Owner has failed to reply to the Notice within 14+1 days.

A Dispute can also arise when the Adjoining Owner is unsure about the proposed works and wishes to engage a Surveyor to look into the proposed in great detail.

Section 10(4) has important implications for Property Owners and Property Managers. Who pays the fees/costs of Party Wall Surveyors and why the system operates in this manner, are issues explained later in this book.

CHAPTER 12

Simplified Process - Adjoining Owner Perspective

Once your neighbour has decided to carry out a project, the process is as follows.

They will create Planning drawings and submit a planning application or a permitted development application.

They should issue you a Party Wall Notice and follow the Party Wall process prior to commencing works. They can begin Non-Notifiable works while the Party Wall process continues.

The Party Wall Process - Overview

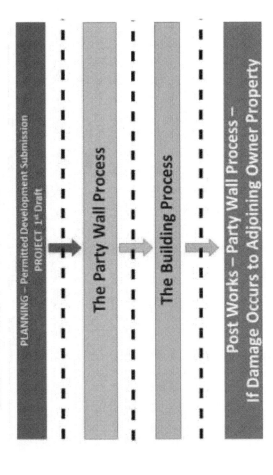

PLANNING – Permitted Development Submission
PROJECT 1ᵈ Draft

The Party Wall Process

The Building Process

Post Works – Party Wall Process –
If Damage Occurs to Adjoining Owner Property

Once the building works are completed, if there is damage and only if there is damage, the post Works process is triggered. This process is out of scope for this book.

The Party Wall process from the Adjoining Owner's perspective starts when the Building Owner Serves the Adjoining Owner Notices as required by The Act.

The Party Wall (PARTY WALL - AO) - Process

Building Serves Notices to (AO)

Adjoining Owner (AO) – Response - Options

| 1. Consent with A Schedule of Condition(SoC) Using Building Owners Surveyor – (BOS) | 2. Agreed Surveyor BO – AO Use Same Surveyor | 3. AO Appoint Own Surveyor | 4. AO – Do Nothing The 10(4) Process |

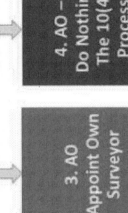

Now you, the Adjoining owner have four response options.

1. Consent with a Schedule of Condition Survey.

2. You can use an Agreed Surveyor which will be the same Surveyor that is appointed by your neighbour.

3. Appoint your own Surveyor.

4. Do nothing and not respond to the Notices, which is actually the worst option for you.

Your Response Option – (AO)
1. Consent - with Schedule of Condition- (SoC)

1. BOS Make Appointment With Adjoining Owner (AO)	**2. Carry – Out Survey on Adjoining Owner's Property**	**3. Produce – Schedule of Condition (Soc) Report**	**4. Send – SoC Report Schedule of Condition To Both Owners – AO & BO**

Option 1. Consent with a Schedule of Condition

If you choose to Consent with a Schedule of Condition then the Building Owner's Surveyor will make an appointment to carry out a Survey of your property prior to the works commencing. The Building Owner Surveyor will produce a Schedule of Condition report and send a copy to both the Adjoining Owner and the Building Owner i.e. send you a copy and send a copy to the people carrying out the works.

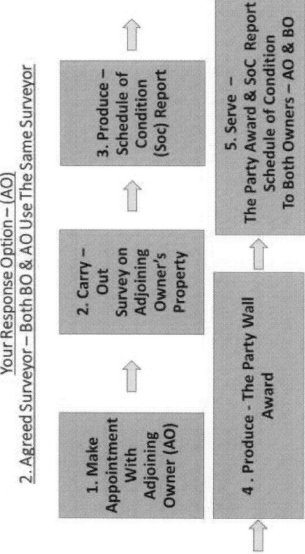

1. Make Appointment With Adjoining Owner (AO)

2. Carry – Out Survey on Adjoining Owner's Property

3. Produce – Schedule of Condition (Soc) Report

4 . Produce - The Party Wall Award

5. Serve – The Party Award & SoC Report Schedule of Condition To Both Owners – AO & BO

Option 2. Agreed Surveyor

The second option is to use an Agreed Surveyor. In this scenario you are using the same Surveyor for both parties. This is permitted under the Act.

Whether this is a good idea or not depends on:
- The project complexity
- The Surveyor being proposed by the Building Owner

You are entitled to use your Surveyor as the Agreed Surveyor, if you wish. This has to be agreed by both parties.

The Agreed Surveyor will make an appointment with you (the Adjoining Owner) to carry out a survey of your property prior to works beginning. They will create a Schedule of Condition Survey report.

In addition, they will produce a legal document called a Party Wall Award. Both documents are Served to both Owners.

1. BO – Appoint Their Own Surveyor (BOS)

2. AO – Appoint Their Own Surveyor (AOS)

3. AOS & BOS Select The Third Surveyor

4. AOS– Organises Appointment for SoC

5. BOS– Carries out SoC

6. BOS – Drafts SoC Report & Draft Party Wall Award

7. AOS – Checks SoC Report & Draft Party Wall Award

Option 3. Appoint Your Own Surveyor

In this instance, the Building Owner and the Adjoining Owner will each appoint their own Surveyor.

The first task for both of these Surveyors is to Select a Third Surveyor, who can be called upon should there be a disagreement between the Surveyors.

Either the Building Owner or the Adjoining Owner can contact the Third Surveyor, should they disagree with anything proposed by either Surveyor.

Next, the Adjoining Owner Surveyor organises an appointment for the Schedule of Condition Survey on your property.

The Building Owner Surveyor and the Adjoining Owner Surveyor would usually carry out this Schedule of Condition together.

The Building Owner Surveyor then drafts a report for the Schedule of Condition and produces a Party Wall Award, which is a legal document setting out the Rights and Responsibilities of both parties.

Your Response Option – (AO)
3. AO – Appoints their Own Surveyor

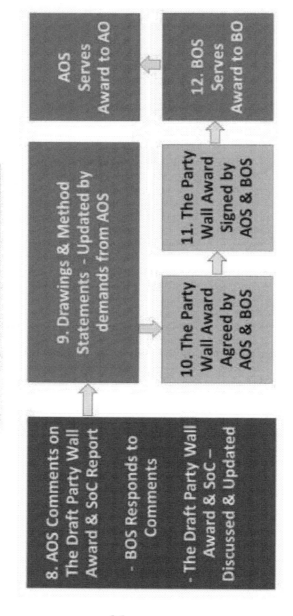

8. AOS Comments on The Draft Party Wall Award & SoC Report

- BOS Responds to Comments

- The Draft Party Wall Award & SoC – Discussed & Updated

9. Drawings & Method Statements - Updated by demands from AOS

10. The Party Wall Award Agreed by AOS & BOS

11. The Party Wall Award Signed by AOS & BOS

AOS Serves Award to AO

12. BOS Serves Award to BO

Option 3. Appoint Your Own Surveyor

The next element of the process is for the Adjoining Owner Surveyor to check this report and the Party Wall Award. It is the Adjoining Owner Surveyor's responsibility to review and comment upon the Award and the Schedule of Condition report.

We would also ask for amendments to the Party Wall Award where we think things have been missed or additional protection is needed.

Usually the amendments requested by us are discussed with the architects and the project planners and we come to an agreement with the Building Owner's Surveyor. These need to be included in the Party Wall Award, which is the legal document.

Again, setting out the Rights and Responsibilities of both parties is something that is agreed between the two Surveyors. Both Surveyors then sign the Party Wall Award.

The Building Owner Surveyor Serves the Award to the Building Owner and your Surveyor, the Adjoining Owner Surveyor will Serve the Award to you.

97

Your Response Option – (AO)
4. AO – Do Nothing The 10(4) Process

| 1. AO – Does NOT reply to Your Notice | → | 2. Send Reminder Letter | → | 3. After 12 Days Still No - Reply | → | 4. Appoint Surveyor – On Behalf of Adjoining Owner |

3.1 AO Reply's by Selecting An Option

1. - Consent With Schedule of Condition- SoC
2. - Agreed Surveyor BO – AO Use Same Surveyor
3. - AO Appoint Own Surveyor

Option 4. Do Nothing / No Response

This is the worst option, which is not to reply to the Notices as a neighbour that may be affected by the works. This should be avoided at all costs if at all possible. Unfortunately the situation is sometimes unavoidable, for example if you are away on holiday or due to some other personal circumstances.

The Building Owner should send you a reminder letter, after 12 days of the reminder letter lapsing.

The Building Owner **MUST** and I repeat **MUST** appoint a Surveyor on your behalf.

We have seen countless number of times where the process is ignored and a Surveyor is not appointed.

Of course, prior to a Surveyor being appointed on your behalf you can still choose the previous three options.

If you received a Party Wall Notice, we recommend that you discuss your issues and concerns with a Surveyor in order to work on the best response. There have been many instances where Adjoining Owners believe that they can frustrate the process by not replying to the Party Wall Notice.

This actually acts against your interest and it is not an opportunity to carry on your planning fight with the neighbours.

CHAPTER 13

Section Six Notice
(AO Perspective)

We will now look at notices required under The Act, specifically Section Six(6) Notice. There are two categories of Section Six(6) Notice; Section Six 6(1) and Section Six 6(2).

For all Section Six 6 Notice works, a minimum of one month's Notice is required. This Notice period can be decreased if the Adjoining Owner who has the right to reject such requests.

If there is no reply to a Section Six(6) Notice within 14+1 days, the Adjoining Owner is Deemed to have dissented.

Under the Deemed Service Act., a notice is Deemed to be Served after one day of postage via the Royal Mail, assuming it has been posted via first class post. It is irrelevant whether a Notice is actually received as long as a Certificate of Posting (CoP) is obtained at time of posting to prove that the letter was indeed posted. By doing this, the Building Owner has carried out the prescribed process and met their obligation.

Section Six 6(1) Notice is used mainly for excavations for Drainage, Rear Extensions and Basements. Section Six 6(1) works are only notifiable if they meet both the following criteria:

- Excavation must be within three metres of the Adjoining Property. This distance is measured horizontally along the ground.

- The depth of the excavation must be lower than that of the Adjoining Owner's foundation, measured Vertically.

The key date to remember here is 1976. Buildings built before 1976 have quite a shallow foundation. Post 1976 to 1980's buildings were built with significantly deeper foundations. The change in building structure was largely due to the change in Building Regulations as a result of the heat wave in the summer of 1976 which led to properties suffering structural damage as a result.

Section Six 6(2) Notices deal with works which are deeper than Section Six 6(1) works and therefore likely to be either commercial works or basements but not exclusively.

The two tests, which need to be met for Section Six 6(2) works to be notifiable are as follows:

- The excavation must be within six metres of the Adjoining Property. This distance is measured horizontally along the ground.

- A slightly more complicated second test compared to Section Six(1). Meet a plane drawn downwards in the direction at an angle of forty-five degrees to the horizontal from the line formed by the intersection of the plane of the level of the bottom of the foundations of the structure of the adjoining owner with the plane of the external face of the external wall structure of the adjoining owner.

Both types of Section Six 6 Notice must be accompanied by drawings/plans showing the depth and the position of the excavations.

CHAPTER 14

Section One Notice (AO Perspective)

We will now look at Section One 1 Notice under The Act. This is also known as the Line of Junction Notice and must be issued one month prior to works commencing; although this can be earlier by agreement of the Adjoining Owner.

Section One (1) Notices allow the Building Owner to gain access to the Adjoining Owner's land and place scaffolding in order to carry out these works.

In order to actually gain access to the Adjoining Owner's land for the purposes of works the Building Owner must also issue a Section Eight 8 Notice.

Most common types of Section One Notice are Section 1(5), Section 1(2) and Section 1(6).

A Section One 1(5) Notice is required when a Building Owner intends to build on the Line of Junction but wholly on their own land.

If the Building Owner is building a wall or a flank wall for a side extension under Section 1(5), the foundations cannot cross onto the Adjoining Owner's land. Therefore, the foundations need to be Eccentric foundations, whereby the wall is constructed on the edge of the foundations.

Section One 1(2) allows the walls/foundations to be built astride the boundary but is subject to the written consent of the Adjoining Owner. Both Owners share this wall whether it's a flank wall or a Party Fence Wall and can be used by the Adjoining Owner at a point in future.

Section One 1(6), is where the Building Owner wants to place foundations on the Adjoining

Owner's land. Again, this is subject to written consent from the Adjoining Owner.

Section One (1) Notices are different to those of Section Six 6 and Section Three 3 in that consent is automatically assumed if there is no reply within 14+1 days. However, this does not mean a Building Owner can issue a Section One 1(2) or a Section One 1(6) Notice and then automatically place footings on the Adjoining Owner's Land. Separate consent must be sought and granted in writing before this can happen.

This is a very important point as placing footings, however small on the Adjoining Owner's Land can constitute an ongoing trespass. This can be very expensive to remedy in terms of both construction costs and high legal fees.

There is no real need to place the footing on the Adjoining Owner's land as this can be designed out by the use of Eccentric footings. Projecting footings are a habit of builders who want to place footings which protect beyond a wall.

Section One (1) Notices can also be used to build a fence which requires little or no foundation.

CHAPTER 15

Section Two/Three Notices (AO Perspective)

These works are defined under Section Two (2) of The Act. However, a Section Three (3) Notice is Served in order to Notify the Adjoining Owners. For the purposes of this discussion, we refer to these works as Section Three (3) works.

The notice period for Section Three (3) works is two months. Of course works can start earlier should the Adjoining Owners agree who has a right to reject such requests. The Adjoining Owners may need to use the Notice period in order to prepare for the works.

A Section Three (3) notice is an automatic dissent Notice whereby if there is no reply from the Adjoining Owners within 14+1 days, it is assumed that they have dissented (Deemed dissent). However, the Building Owner cannot go ahead and start works. They must follow the Section 10(4) process, as defined under Section 10(4) of The Act which is discusses later in this book

Section Three (3) Notice works Notify the Adjoining Owner of works to the Party Wall and these include the following:

- Removal of Chimney Breasts which are the elements of the Chimney underneath the Roof Line.
- Chimney Stacks can also be removed but this needs the written consent of the Adjoining Owners.

- Loft Conversions where Steel is inserted into the Party Wall in order to create separation to meet Acoustic requirements .
- Raising the Party Wall to form cheeks of a Loft Conversion (the flank walls).
- A Party Fence Wall can be raised in the rear garden, which extended for use as the flank Wall for a Rear Extension.

Raising a Party Fence Wall to incorporate within a Rear Extension can be a good idea for both Building Owners and future Adjoining Owners, as this saves space and costs. However, the second Owner to make use of the wall will need to pay the first Owner enclosure costs subject to Section11(11). This is discussed in detail in the "Wall Astride the Boundary" chapter in this book.

CHAPTER 16

Section 10(4)

Look at The Act Section10 covers the resolution of disputes, sub-section four (4) is very important and its implication for Property Owners.

For Building Owners and the Adjoining Owners, Section 10(4) covers the non-response to a Party Wall Notice. This applies where an Adjoining Owner fails/refuses to Appoint a Surveyor.

In a scenario where the Building Owner Serves the Adjoining Owner a Notice. The Adjoining Owner upon receiving a Notice feels unhappy with the works being proposed and decides not to respond to the Notice.

This may be a tactic used to try and delay the works. The Act is an enabling Act. One of the purposes of The Act is   to enable building works to take place, as well as, to afford Adjoining Owners to protect their property. Hence keep both parties out of court.

Section 10 is designed to ensure that the whole process keeps moving.

Other reasons for non-response may also be,

- They have forgotten or
- They are busy,

Once a Notice is sent out by the Building Owner.

14 days after a lack of response the Building Owner, should send out another letter known as a reminder/10(4) Letter within the industry. This gives

the Adjoining Owners a further 10 days to respond to the original Notice.

If there is no response to this reminder letter.

The Building Owner, **MUST** I repeat, **MUST** appoint a Surveyor on the Adjoining Owner's behalf.

As an Adjoining Owner, failure to respond to a Notice used theoretically mean a Surveyor will be Appointed on your behalf. However, this is not always the case.

We've come across numerous cases, where the Adjoining Owners have not responded and no Surveyor under Section 10(4)(b) has been appointed on behalf of the Adjoining Owner. Either because the Building Owner Surveyor doesn't know the rules, or the Building Owner has not authorised their Surveyor to Appointed Surveyor on his behalf in order to try and save costs.

We have also come across a number of professional advisers including Lawyers, Architects and other parties who do not understand this is the process they should be carrying out.

It is the duty of the Building Owner to follow this process through. If they do not, they are still Legally obligated to allow a Surveyor for the Adjoining Surveyor to be appointed.

In terms of an Adjoining

Here is the 10(4) rule explained again.
- After 14 days of Serving a Notice.
- If there is no response. The next step is to send a reminder letter to the Adjoining Owner giving a further 10 days to reply.
- If there is no reply, after this period the Building Owner must appoint a different Surveyor for their Adjoining Owner.

This is to ensure that the Adjoining Owner is independently represented and to ensure that both parties the Building and Adjoining Owner have their own Surveyors representing their interests.

The original purpose behind this rule is to ensure that the process is kept moving. To stop the process from being frustrated by the Adjoining Owners and not to allow the Adjoining Owners to stop the works by simply not replying to the Party Wall Notice.

If the Adjoining Owner fails to respond to a Letter known as a reminder Letter. The Building Owner is under a duty to Appoint a Surveyor on behalf of the Adjoining Owner.

The 10(4) reminder Letter as it is known, lapses after 10 days, usually one/two days are added to ensure that the Serve period is taken into account. The costs of the Adjoining Owners will follow the protocols of the Act for apportioning Surveyors costs. The protocol of who benefits from the works follows that where you have work such as a Loft Conversion, Extension, Removal of Chimney or a Basement; in all of these cases, the benefit accrues entirely to the Building Owner. The Adjoining owner gains no benefit, hence the Adjoining Owner's surveys costs will be borne by the Building Owner.

However, where you have work such as repairing shared walls, shared Party Walls or repairing Chimney Stacks, which are shared by several owners it is unfair that the entire costs are borne by the owner instituting the works. As an Adjoining Owner you have the right to have your own Party Wall Surveyor, or one will be appointed on your behalf. If you are going to have a Party Wall Surveyor, you might as well have one who specialises in this area. If you receive a Notice as an Adjoining Owner, have a look carefully at who the Building Owner is proposing to use as a Surveyor.

It is up to you to respond within the time limits. Failure to respond can lead to problems. You

Surveyor will be able to advise you. If you have any special requirements, which may include being a tenant, being visually impaired, or requiring extra access; these may be able to be accommodated within the Method statements and the conditions set up within the Award.

There are a number of times when you come across Adjoining Owners who've had no Surveyors appointed on their behalf, by the Building Owner whether that's done deliberately by the Building Owner in order to save costs or whether they do not know the process.

Building Owners, Surveyors, Architects or Lawyers may not understand the rule fully. The Building Surveyor who Serves the Notice may have been mis-informed by the Building Owner.

Or, the Building Owner may have refused to authorise the Building Owner Surveyor to appoint the Adjoining Owner Surveyor. Whatever the reason, maybe to save costs.

Therefore, by implication, you may not have any Surveyor representing you as an Adjoining Owner.

There may not be an Award in place; there may be an Unagreed Surveyor representing your interest and looking at issues involved in the works; there may even be no Surveyors to deal with any post works damage issues.

CHAPTER 17

Who is a Building Owner

Looking at the major definitions under The Act. Firstly, we'll look at the definition for a Building Owner.

The Building Owner is defined as an owner who wishes to exercise his rights under the Act to carry out notifiable works. Building Owners can, of course, include freeholders and leaseholders.

A very important point to note and understand here, is that Leaseholders will need to obtain the necessary permissions from the freeholder.

However, there are strategies for starting the Party Wall process and pausing until the freeholder consents are finalised.

Definitions of Adjoining Owners under The Act include:

- Anyone entitled to see all or part profits from the land.
- A person in possession of the land otherwise than a mortgagee i.e. mortgage companies excluded
- As tenants from year to year or a lesser term or as a tenant at will. So, therefore assured short tenancies are excluded however long leaseholders are one of the notifiable owners.

An important point to note here leaseholders under seven years are not required to register the lease with the land registry. Therefore, this group is sometimes missed out; leaseholders with leases of less than 7 years but greater then one year are also notifiable Adjoining Owners.

Another group, of course, is anyone who is under contract to buy the land, and therefore has an interest in the land.

It is entirely possible to have more than One Adjoining Owner for one piece of land i.e. it is possible to have the following Adjoining Owners

- Freeholders

- Leaseholders

- and if the property is contracted to sell; the new owners

CHAPTER 18

Adjoining Owner: Definition of Adjoining Owner

Look at the important definitions and The Act. One of the most important definitions is who qualifies as an Adjoining Owner.

- A person who is entitled to receive all or part of rents or profits from land.

- The person who is in possession of land this excludes mortgage companies, also excludes tenants with leases of less than a year i.e. short hold tenants.

- Anyone under contract to purchase land.

Although there are three groups listed in The Act, this actually represents four categories of Adjoining Owners:

(i)   Freeholders

(ii)   Anyone entitled to receive rental

(iii)   Anyone contracted to buy the land

(iv)   Leaseholders

Therefore, it is possible to have a situation, where the property has been exchanged on property and the contract has not yet completed.

Hence, both the previous owner and the new exchanged owners are both notifiable owners. Once the contract completes, the old owner falls away and the new owner remains as the Adjoining Owner.

Properties can also have Leaseholders, it is entirely possible for an Adjoining property to more than one owner Notifiable owner. The most common examples being where; the flat owners are notifiable as Leasehold owners and also the Freehold owners of the entire building.

Each of the Leaseholders and Freeholders can select their own server individually. Adjoining owners include leasehold owners but do not include shorthold tenancies or council tenants.

An important issue to pay attention to here. Leaseholds with leases under seven years do not need to be registered with the Land Registry, therefore, these cannot ascertained by Surveyors issuing Party Wall Notices to Adjoining Owners.

Commercial Leaseholders usually have a self-repairing lease, which makes the leaseholders responsible for the maintenance of parts of the property. This class of Leaseholder may miss out.

Therefore, when the freeholder received notice, they should inform the Surveyor serving the notice of any such leaseholders.

For residential works, both leaseholders of flats and the freeholders need to be notified. With flat

Leaseholders, short leases are less than seven years or less of a problem. It is more of an issue where you have commercial leases of seven years or less.

Other issues affecting residential works include the Adjoining Owners may be selling their property, so that new owners are notifiable, as soon as they are under contract.

Residential flat Leaseholder, wanting to carry out notifiable works will also need to get the license to alter. The license to alter and the Party Wall process are quite different processes. It may be better to deal with the license to alter prior to undertaking the Party Wall process.

The Building Owner is simply an owner who desires to execute their rights under the Act to carry out notifiable works. Usually, there is only one Building Owner either Leaseholder or the Freeholder who is going to undertake the works. Therefore, on that side, it is quite simple.

CHAPTER 19

Party Wall Surveyors Fees-Who Pays & Why.

We will now look at who pays for the Party Wall Surveyor's fees.

This is a very good question and it is important to dispel a myth that "the Building Owner always pays the fees".

This myth is not entirely true to investigate this further we will look at Section 10 of the Act "An award may determine—"

Section 10(12)(c) of the Act.
"any other matter arising out of or incidental to the dispute including the costs of making the award;"

Under "any other matters arising out of or incidental to the dispute including the costs of making the ward" are settled by the Surveyors by the means of an Award.

In other words, it is the Surveyor/s, who determine who pay their fees. The convention followed here:
- "Fees are apportioned to the Owner/s who benefit from the Works".

So, where notifiable works benefit several owners the cost of those works are apportioned in relation to who benefits from the works.

A classic example is, where a chimney which is shared by several owners is being repaired. It is only fair that all Adjoining Owners contribute towards the costs of the repair of the Chimney and to the Surveyor's costs.

Another example may be where several owners share internal or external walls.

There are projects where the entire benefit gained by the works solely accrue to the Building Owners, examples include Basements.

In addition, looking at Loft conversations, the whole of the benefits accrues to the Building Owner, hence the Adjoining Owners Surveyor's fees are entirely paid by the Building Owner.

In the case of Rear Extensions, the entire benefits accrue to the Building Owner. Hence, the Building Owner pays the whole of the Adjoining Owners Surveyor's fees.

Lastly but not least is an example of Chimney Breast being removed, where the whole benefit accrues to the Building Owner i.e. they will gain the extra few feet from removing the Chimney Breast.

The Adjoining Owner has nothing to gain from these works. It is only right and fair that the Building Owner pays the Adjoining Owner Surveyor's costs/fees.

CHAPTER 20

Who Can be a Party Wall Surveyor?

We will now look at one of the most important definitions under The Act and that is of a Party Wall Surveyor. Under Section of The Act a Party Wall Surveyor is defined as:

"surveyor" – " means any person not being a party to the matter appointed or selected under section 10 to determine disputes in accordance with the procedures set out in this Act."

Owners are not allowed to act for themselves in matters of their own property. Therefore, the two people in the world who cannot be a Party Wall Surveyor are:

(1)   The Building Owner and

(2)   The Adjoining Owner

Hence, Surveyors, who own the property or professionals within the Party Wall industry and are unable to act for themselves. They will need to appoint a Surveyor on their behalf.

Usually Party Surveyors have some professional qualification, not only is knowledge and understanding of the construction industry required but also specifically understanding of the Party Wall Law.

The Royal Institute of Chartered Surveyors (RICS) is most commonly recognised by members of the general public. There is a belief that only Chartered Surveyors can be Party wall Surveyors, this is incorrect.

The other body fast gaining a reputation for its members having high standards of knowledge and experience in Party Wall matters is the Faculty of Party Wall Surveyors. Members of the Faculty Party Wall Surveyors are highly respected within the Party Wall Surveying industry.

The Faculty is a non-profit making organisation, whose mission is to train all Surveyors in the specific area of Party Wall Surveying.

You may or may not have noticed that many members of the RICS organisation are also members of Faculty of Party Wall Surveyors due to its excellent training.

What should you be looking for if you are trying to engage a Party Wall Surveyor ?

Try to ensure that your Surveyor is a member of a training organisation such as Royal Institute of Chartered Surveyors (RICS) or the Faculty of Party Wall Surveyors.

What else should you be looking for?

You will often see generalist Surveyors who do general Surveying and who also do Party Wall Surveying on the side. More and more frequently there are Specialist Party Wall Surveyors who specialise in Party Wall Surveying.

Of course, they should carry Professional Indemnity Insurance to protect you.

Continuing Professional Development, CPD is quite important in this area as it is quite a recent field that is fast developing. There are a number of cases being decided in the courts which are affecting how things are done.

You may wish to ask the question, what sort of CPD does your Surveyor undertake?

This is not an extensive list, but it is the most obvious things. You may of course think of other questions related to your project.

CHAPTER 21

Third Surveyor

We will now look at one of the most important definitions under The Act, one of the roles that causes the most confusion, that of the Third Surveyor.

There is a huge misunderstanding of the Role of a Third Surveyor. Owners nearly always get this wrong and mixed up.

In a situation is where we have two Surveyors, so that there is a Surveyor for the Building Owner and the Adjoining Owner wishes to appoint their own Surveyor, as is their right. One of the first duties of the two Surveyors is to select a Third Surveyor. All three are referred to as The Three Surveyors.

The Third Surveyor has a very specific role and they are generally not called upon unless one of the following issues occurs: Either of the Surveyors or either of the Parties to a dispute call upon the Third Surveyor to determine disputed matters. Then they shall make the necessary Award. Making an Award is the process whereby the dispute is settled.

In the case of two Surveyors disagreeing with each other on a technical or procedural issue. One of the Surveyors can call upon the Third Surveyor to make a discussion similar to a judgement by a Judge. The Building Owner or the Adjoining Owner can also call upon the Third Surveyor to make a judgement on an issue or an item, which is outstanding. Either of the owners may also call upon the Third Surveyor, if they believe their appointed Surveyor's handling of any particular issue is incorrectly.

There is a common misunderstanding, which is largely mistaken by Building Owners. Building Owners often believe they have to pay a Third Surveyor to be also involved.

Third Surveyor's fees only accrue or/are charged when they are called upon to deal with a specific issue. In addition, the costs are levied against the party found to be incorrect.

So, for example, the Adjoining Surveyor may be handling a particular issue incorrectly. The Building Owner may call upon the Third Surveyor, if the Third Surveyor finds that the Adjoining Surveyor is dealing with the matter incorrectly.

Third Surveyors costs may be awarded against the Adjoining Owners. Therefore, it is quite important for Adjoining Owners and Adjoining Surveyors to understand the extent of their role, and not to treat this as a blank chequebook.

One of the most common issues settled by the Third Surveyor is that of Adjoining Owner Surveyor's fees and if it goes against the Adjoining Surveyor; the Adjoining Owner could end up paying The Third Surveyor fees.

CHAPTER 22 –

The Resolution of Disputes

We will now look at Section 10 of The Act which contains the dispute resolution procedure. Whether a dispute is deemed, which means there was no reply to the initial notice. Or if the dispute has occurred by the Adjoining Owner writing to the Building Owner saying that they're in dispute and they wish to appoint either an Agreed Surveyor as or their own Surveyor in order to resolve the dispute.

A dispute is resolved by means of an Award, which is prepared by the Surveyors or the Agreed Surveyor.

An Award can only refer to notifiable works under the Act. It is a legal document, which determines the Right to execute works, the time and manner in which those notifiable works will be executed. So, that you may get restrictions on working hours with noisy notifiable works. Method statements minimise the probability of risk to the Adjoining Owner's property.

A classic Method statement is that of "hit and miss" foundations, whereby foundations are dug out in sections. One metre to 1.20m metres, alternating so that the risk of subsidence to Adjoining Owner's property is minimised.

Another items determined in the Award is the cost of making the Award.

The Surveyor's fees/costs seem to be a common misconception, that the Building Owner always pays for both the Surveyor's fees; this is not actually the case. All the surveyor's fees are portioned to who actually benefits from the works proposed.

So, for work such as

- Loft Conversions
- Rear extensions
- Chimney breasts
- Basements

Where Building Owner accrue all the benefits and hence it is only fair that they pay for all the Surveyor's fees.

However, in case of works for repairs, an example being a Chimney Stack whose repair has been neglected and is shared by a number of owners. You may have an instance where the Chimney Stack is shared by a house on one side and two flats on the other side, hence a number of owners will benefit from the repair of the Chimney Stack.

Regardless of who actually serves the Notice to instigates the works. It is only fair that the all costs of both the works and the Surveyors are split between the three owners. A better approach may be to get advice before appointing Surveyors or agreeing to their appointment.

CHAPTER 23

Wall Astride the Boundary

The Act Section11(11) states "Where use is subsequently made by the Adjoining Owner of work carried out solely at the expense of the Building Owner, the Adjoining Owner shall pay a due proportion of the expenses incurred by the Building Owner in carrying out that work; and for this purpose he shall be taken to have incurred expenses calculated by reference to what the cost of the work would be if it were carried out at the time when that subsequent use is made."

The Basic Concept / Mistakes Made by Owners when making an agreement between themselves.

Owners can agree anything they like between themselves. Following the process outlined below will help both owners from getting themselves into disagreement and dispute as work progresses.

On the whole, building a Wall astride the Boundary is a good idea as it saves costs and more importantly saves space for both owners; for example sharing one cavity flank wall instead of both owners building their own.

Care needs to be taken as this can potentially lead to a boundary dispute developing as well as arguments over the cost of the wall.

Surveyors have to be guided by The Act which sets out the position. The following process is likely to be followed by the Surveyors if they are engaged.

Once both neighbours have agreed to share a flank wall of an extension i.e., the side wall, the following process should be followed.

The first owner to build produces drawings for the design of their proposed extension. They should issue their neighbour a Party Wall Notice under Section 1 (2), "subject to your written consent it is intended to build on the line of junction of the said lands a party wall." Ideally, and especially if a Section Six(6) Notice is also required, this needs to accompanied by drawings showing the position and depth of drawings.

Note that the first owner, in this case the Building Owner needs to obtain written consent to place the wall on the Adjoining Owners land. Along with this consent it is a good idea to name the Surveyor who will be used by both parties in case a dispute develops at some point. A Sample agreement is attached in the Appendices at the end of this book.

The height of the Party wall is important as this needs to be sufficient for owners' projects i.e., if one is building a flat roof and the other is using a tiled roof, the wall heights required will differ.

Once position and height of the Wall is Agreed, Ideally this should be marked on the ground and wall with indelible paint/spray beyond the intended so that everyone is clear where the wall will be built. This will also help to avoid causing Boundary disputes in the future.

There may be a time lag between the first owner building their extension and the second owner building theirs.   It is only fair and right that the second owners pay the first owner for making use of the newly built wall. This is covered under the Act by Section 11(11) commonly and incorrectly called "Enclosure Costs". This is where the first owner to build the Party Wall pays for the full building cost and the second owner pays a portion of the cost when they use a section of the wall as part of their extension. The calculation for cost payable by the second owner is calculated in the following manner:

Half of cost of Area Used, based on the costs at the time of making use of the wall.

Sometimes the second owner pays the first owner at the time of building the wall the amount quoted by builders who are building this extension. This figure is likely to differ from that calculated by Surveyors. Whilst this practice is acceptable, it is advisable to pay for the wall at point of use as plans can invariably change. The costs will be based at the time of building therefore may be higher than had the costs been paid at the time of the build.

The wall is a Party Wall by the virtue of its position; therefore future owners can make use of this Party Wall.

CHAPTER 24

Architects – What to look for when undertaking a Survey

When architects conduct a Survey in order to produce a design scheme, the following additional data collection will be a help to when producing the Party Wall Notices and may prevent having to go back to the site in order to work out the Notifiable Owners.

Please see Appendix for examples of templates for the checklist / Survey sheet.

CHAPTER 25

Developers – What to Look for

The liability in a Party Wall Award stays live for perpetuity and goes with the ownership of a property. An example of this is loft conversions and removal of chimneys by the Building Owner. On the other side the Party Wall may be lined by cupboards or wardrobes. Any damage is only discovered when these cupboards are removed at a later date by the Adjoining Owner. In this case the current Building Owners are liable for the damage caused by the previous Building Owners.

The Right to execute works under Party Wall Awards are individual to the owners and NOT transferable with a property. Therefore, if a developer buys a development where the Party Wall Awards are in place, these Awards are null and void as far as the new owner is concerned. Although the Party Wall Process needs to be restarted and new Awards produced, there is some advantage in that you could use the previous Surveyors as the neighbours are more likely to re-engage in the process as they will have dealt with them previously.

When designing a scheme Section Six(6)(1) or (2) are quite easy to deal with. Section One(1) are most useful sections for developments enabling scaffolding to be erected on the Adjoining Owner's land without having to pay for a scaffolding Licences for the works in pursuance of The Act.

Section Three (3) / Two (2) causes the most problems; which range from:

- Incorrect assumptions about the construction of the Building Owner's building.
- Unknown conditions and make-up of the Adjoining Owner's building.

The first time a designer of a scheme discovers the make-up of the Building Owner's building construction is when they survey the site for the purposes of drawing up a scheme. This requires care to be taken when recording the details of the current construction.

In the case of commercial projects, where there is a Party Wall or the Adjoining Owner's wall foundation can be ascertained from the Building Owner's land it is still worth digging trial holes in order to ascertain the construction of their foundation. Although, technically these trial holes may be notifiable via a Notice; usually informing the neighbour's Surveyor is sufficient.

Access to someone with understanding, knowledge and the implications of The Act can prove invaluable, both in terms of what to do and also what may be possible under the Rights given to Building Owners under The Act.

Alongside the Rights to place Scaffolding on the Adjoining Owner's Land under Section 1(5) and Section 8, Section Two/Three also gives Rights under Sections 2(2)(g) and 2(2)(h) quoted below for reference. These give rights to:

Sections 2(2)(g) "cut away from a party wall, party fence wall, external wall or boundary wall any footing or any projecting chimney breast, jamb or flue, or other projection on or over the land of the Building Owner in order to erect, raise or underpin any such wall or for any other purpose;"

Sections 2(2)((h) "cut away or demolish parts of any wall or building of an Adjoining Owner overhanging the land of the building owner or overhanging a party wall, to the extent that it is necessary to cut away or demolish the parts to enable a vertical wall to be erected or raised against the wall or building of the adjoining owner"

The second unknown is the construction and make-up of the Adjoining Owner's building. The first time anyone sees the make-up of the Adjoining Owner's building may be at the time of the Schedule of Condition survey.

In general, being flexible, willing to re-design the scheme and having knowledge of the Rights given to Building Owners under The Act can prove invaluable.

In the case of development projects, there can be a trade-off between compliance costs of a Method Statement and the value added to the development by extra square footage being gained. There are also the costs of waiting time to start the project while the Party Wall matters are concluded.

Examples of where the Building Owners have not been able to build according to their designs are quite rare but have included a project where the Building Owners were unable to remove a Chimney Breast due to the next door house having asbestos in the Chimney. This would have disturbed the Asbestos and made Health and Safety compliance difficult.

APPENDICES

Appendix A –

Glossary of Terms:

These are most commonly used terms, where the definitions under Section 20 Interpretations are given in the Act and reproduced below.

- "**adjoining owner**" and "**adjoining occupier**" respectively mean any owner and any occupier of land, buildings, storeys or rooms adjoining those of the building owner and for the purposes only of section 6 within the distances specified in that section;

- "**appointing officer**" means the person appointed under this Act by the local authority to make such appointments as are required under section 10(8);

- "**building owner**" means an owner of land who is desirous of exercising rights under this Act;

- "**foundation**", in relation to a wall, means the solid ground or artificially formed support resting on solid ground on which the wall rests;

- "**owner**" includes—

(a) a person in receipt of, or entitled to receive, the whole or part of the rents or profits of land;

(b) a person in possession of land, otherwise than as a mortgagee or as a tenant from year to year or for a lesser term or as a tenant at will;

(c) a purchaser of an interest in land under a contract for purchase or under an agreement for a lease, otherwise than under an agreement for a tenancy from year to year or for a lesser term;

These three categories actually map onto four categories:

(i) Freeholders,

(ii) Anyone entitled to receive rental or profits

(iii) Anyone contracted to buy the land

(iv) Leaseholders

- **"party fence wall"** means a wall (not being part of a building) which stands on lands of different owners and is used or constructed to be used for separating such adjoining lands, but does not include a wall constructed on the land of one owner the artificially formed support of which projects into the land of another owner;

- **"party structure"** means a party wall and also a floor partition or other structure separating buildings or parts of buildings approached solely by separate staircases or separate entrances;

- **"party wall"** means—

   (a) a wall which forms part of a building and stands on lands of different owners to a greater extent than the projection of any artificially formed support on which the wall rests; and

(b) so much of a wall not being a wall referred to in paragraph (a) above as separates buildings belonging to different owners;

- "**special foundations**" means foundations in which an assemblage of beams or rods is employed for the purpose of distributing any load; and

- "**surveyor**" means any person not being a party to the matter appointed or selected under section 10 to determine disputes in accordance with the procedures set out in this Act.

Although, not defined in the Section 20 Section 10 has some definitions, which are useful.

Third Surveyor: - Section10(1)(b) each party shall appoint a surveyor and the two surveyors so appointed shall forthwith select a third surveyor (all of whom are in this section referred to as "the three surveyors").

Appointments: Section10(2) All appointments and selections made under this section shall be in writing and shall not be rescinded by either party.

Appendix B –

New wall Astride the Boundary
Acknowledgment of Line of Junction Notice.

To (Building Owner):

_____

Of (Building Owner's main address):

_____

The Party Wall etc Act 1996 ("the Act")
Acknowledgment of Notice

As Adjoining Owners under the Act of

Adjoining Owner's building:

_____ and having

received notices

dated _____ in respect of proposed works at

Building Owner's building:

_____ and without

prejudice to any of our rights under the Act,

We Adjoining Owner:

Consent for you to build a Party Wall astride the boundary between our properties as proposed in your notice.

In the event of a dispute arising under the Act:

We would concur in the appointment of Agreed Surveyor Mr Dil Gujral BA(Hons) MFPWS to act as an agreed surveyor if required.

Yours sincerely

Building Owner:

Signed:

_____Date:_____

_____

Name:

_____
_____Print name/s

Signed:

_____Date:_____

_____

Name:

_____
_____Print name/s

Adjoining Owner:

Signed:

_____Date:_____

_____

Name:

_____
_____Print name/s

Signed:

_____Date:_____

_____

Name:

_____
_____Print name/s

Please note all joint owners should sign, also print
your name/s and date the letter.

Appendix C

Architects – Survey for Party Wall Notices

Site Address:	
Project Type	
	Single Storey Rear Extension Double Storey Rear Extension Single Storey Side Extension Double Storey Side Extension Loft Extension/Conversion Basement Porch Chimney Removal Other Works Other Works Details:
Works Property:	Terrace House Semi-Detached House Detached House Ground Floor Flat Mid Flat Loft Flat Other:

Notifiable Left Side Neighbour as viewed from the front	
No. (If flats, flat no at Top)	
Description	Terrace House Semi-Detached House Detached House Ground Floor Flat Mid Flat Loft Flat Other:
Horizontal Distance:	- Attached - 3.0M or less - 6.0M or less - 6.0M or greater
Sheds: Is there a Shed with a Foundation or Floor Slab with 3.0M or 6.0M of proposed excavation	- Attached - 3.0M or less - 6.0M or less 6.0M or greater

Notifiable Right Side Neighbour as viewed from the front	
No. (If flats, flat no at Top)	
Description	Terrace House Semi-Detached House Detached House Ground Floor Flat Mid Flat Loft Flat Other:
Horizontal Distance:	- Attached - 3.0M or less - 6.0M or less - 6.0M or greater
Sheds: Is there a Shed with a Foundation or Floor Slab with 3.0M or 6.0M of proposed excavation	- Attached - 3.0M or less - 6.0M or less - 6.0M or greater

Printed in Great Britain
by Amazon